Colorado's

Most Haunted

A Ghostly Guide to the
Rocky Mountain State

Sandy Arno Lyons

EAGLE VALLEY LIBRARY DISTRICT
P.O. BOX 240   600 BROADWAY
EAGLE, CO 81631   (970) 328-8800

Copyrighted by Sandy Lyons
All rights reserved. No part of this book may be used or reproduced without prior written permission from the publisher, except in the case of brief quotations embedded in critical reviews and articles.

Manufactured in the
United States of America
Copyright 2011

Author: Sandy Arno Lyons
Editor: Dr. Susan Richardson
Photographers: Brenton Curtis & Sandy Arno Lyons
Photo Consultant: Curve Detroit
Cover Design: Tom Zahner-Curve Detroit

SkateRight Publishing
First Edition 2011

Library of Congress Control Number: 2011906384

ISBN 978-0-9798876-1-1

Acknowledgments:

A special thanks to everyone that willingly took part in this exciting project. Without you this book would not have been possible.

Specifically:

Anton, Anton's Publishing Primer

Amy & Tom, CurveDetroit.com

George & Dan, Grand Imperial Hotel

Susan & Amy, Hotel St. Nicholas

Walter & Dee, Lumber Baron Inn

Lynn & Ben, Hotel Boulderado

Adriana, Tony & Jodi, Hotel Jerome

Cheri, Nicole, Sue & Katie, Redstone Inn & Castle

Dean, Aspen Historical Society

Gail, Breckenridge Heritage Alliance

Michael, Bryan & Nanci, Historic Brown Hotel

A Few Words of Thanks:

To my amazing parents, Barb and Mike Arno, and my sister, Amy MacIntosh, for listening to all my crazy ideas and never letting me give up on my dreams.

To my loving husband, Chris, for being the current recipient of my crazy ideas and for supporting me no matter what.

To the greatest daughter in the world, Avery, for letting Mommy get one more thing done.

To my students at Figure Skating Club of Birmingham and New Edge Figure Skating Club for allowing me to do what I love: you inspire me every day.

Dedicated to those in search of the unknown

"I see dead people"
> The Sixth Sense, 1999

"I ain't afraid of no ghost"
> Ghostbusters, 1984

I wasn't sure which quotation was more appropriate. What can I say? I'm a believer with a sense of humor.

Table of Contents

Foreword   1

The Ones That Got Away   5

Hotel Jerome, Aspen   7
    Little Boy Lost   11
    The Other Woman   13
    A Proper Hello   16
    Dog's Day   18

Hotel Boulderado, Boulder   19
    Time to Shut the Door   24
    The Chief Politely Declines   26
    Father-Son Dynamic   28
    I Didn't Just See That   30
    Mezzanine Mystery Man   32
    A Lady Always Flushes Twice   33

Historic Brown, Breckenridge   35
    Bam, Bam, Bam, Bam   38
    3 Hot Spots, 1 Creepy Photo   41

Hotel St. Nicholas, Cripple Creek   45
    Petey   48
    The Quiet Observer   51
    The Angelic Light   53

Lumber Baron Inn & Gardens, Denver 57
   Stares from the Staircase   60
   Room within a Room   62
   A Sad Anniversary   66
   Justice for Cara & Marianne   68
   The Accidental EVP   69

Redstone Inn, Redstone   71
   A Beer for Spirits   74
   The Lone Soldier   76
   Night Whispers   77
   Third Floor Fiesta   79

Redstone Castle, Redstone   81
   Blast from the Past   84
   Cigar, Cigar, Wherever You Are   86

Grand Imperial Hotel, Silverton   89
   The Sad Story of Luigi Regalia   95
   Four Ghosts and a Spider   98
   A Titanic Connection   102

Colorado Map   103

About the Author   104

Foreword

My first book, *Michigan's Most Haunted: A Ghostly Guide to the Great Lakes State*, was such a success that I decided to travel to the great state of Colorado for my second. The Old West did not disappoint with fascinating stories of mining towns, brothels, gambling, and shootouts.

Once again my research started online. Since my first book was published in 2007, there are many more TV shows, websites, blogs, and online magazines dedicated to all things ghostly. I thought for sure this would make finding individuals with firsthand accounts a lot easier.

After all, a magazine or newspaper article on a haunted hotel would certainly check the facts of a story, right? Wrong! The lack of integrity in the media makes every journalistic bone in my body cringe.

Obviously, none of these stories can be proven scientifically, but certain facts of a story can be checked simply by going to the source. Case in point, when I contacted The Baldpate Inn in Estes Park, CO, the owner said she'd love to be in my book but has never seen any ghosts and didn't know of anyone personally that I could talk to. Fair enough.

Months later I came across an online magazine article dated January 2011 detailing recent hauntings at the Baldpate Inn. So I emailed the owner again referencing the article and author. The article claimed firsthand accounts of drinks being spilled off the bar and cigarettes being taken when no one was around.

The owner replied, "I don't know this person, must be a guest; she's not a former employee. Since I hire all seasonal [summer] staff, there's not really anyone around to talk to [It was fall/winter when we corresponded]. I do sort of laugh when I see the stories about spilled drinks (we don't have a bar that serves mixed drinks) or missing cigarettes (we haven't allowed smoking since we bought the place in 1986). So I believe some of these stories are folklore from days long gone."

Folklore from days long gone being presented as fact? I think I just heard my journalism professor at Michigan State roll over in his grave. Roll back over, professor: I can assure you that I got as close to the source as possible for each and every story.

Perhaps I got a little too close. I had my first unexplained experience, albeit unintentional, while researching the Lumber Baron Inn and Gardens in Denver (see "The Accidental EVP," page 69).

My second experience was during my stay at the Hotel St. Nicholas in Cripple Creek, CO, the night before my interview with the owner. I kept popping up in my bed because I thought someone was watching me. I wish I would have had the interview before I spent the night as then I would have known that the property used to be inhabited by nuns, who still watch over the place (see "The Angelic Light," page 53). I'm sure I would have had a better night's sleep.

I hope you have as much fun reading and visiting the places in this book as I did researching and writing it.

Happy Hauntings,
Sandy

P.S. As many of you know, the official state nickname for Colorado is the Centennial State. However, after conducting an unscientific Facebook survey, I found that 100% of the respondents answered, "Colorado" to my question: Which state is the Rocky Mountain State? Even my friends from Colorado. So there :)

The Ones That Got Away

Denver, Colorado
Luxury boutique hotel, downtown:

According to newspaper articles and a local ghost tour, they are haunted by a spirit that would order a drink then disappear once the drink was delivered. No one at the hotel would go on the record; instead they directed me to newspaper articles as my only source. Either talk to me or you're out of the book. They're out.

Glenwood Springs, Colorado
Historic presidential hotel in town:

Management confirmed that they had unexplained events, for example, lavender perfume would float down the hallway when no one was around. After the idea of being in my book was presented to the owners, my phone calls and emails went unreturned. Silence speaks volumes.

Ouray, Colorado
Beautiful old hotel in town:

A local magazine article said the hotel is haunted by a bride who died on her wedding night on the third floor. When I asked the owner about it, there was a long, uncomfortable pause. Then he said, "We don't really go there in our advertising." And that was that.

Denver, Colorado
Large, elite hotel, downtown:

The internet details how a socialite lived at the hotel in the 1940s & 50s in room 904. Years later during history tours, the hotel told her story of heartbreak over lost loves. During the tours the switchboard would light up with calls from room 904 even though at the time the property was being renovated, and room 904 had no electricity or phone. The story was eventually eliminated from the tour, and the calls stopped.

My initial research showed the hotel offered ghost tours on Wednesdays and Saturdays. I thought for sure I had another property for my book. When I asked the hotel historian about it, she said, "Management is not supportive." But they give ghost tours! When I checked the website again, the ghost tour was changed to a history tour "where we recount interesting anecdotes about the general history of the hotel." Way to cover your butt!

Hotel Jerome
Aspen, Colorado

Hoteljerome.com   (877) 412-ROCK

History

The Hotel Jerome was founded by former Union Civil War soldier Jerome B. Wheeler. He was the president of Macy's Department Stores before moving to Aspen in 1883. He built the Hotel Jerome in 1889 to rival the extravagant hotels in Paris and London. He wanted to bring some luxury to the Wild West.

Hotel Jerome   Aspen

Wheeler built it, and the rich and famous soon followed. Decision makers of the day made the Hotel Jerome the epicenter of Aspen's commercial and social life. This modern marvel was one of the first buildings west of the Mississippi to have electricity, hot and cold running water, steam heat, and an elevator.

The grand hotel featured 90 guest rooms, 15 bathrooms, and the famous J-Bar. The popular watering hole had miners bellying up to its cherry wood bar until the silver bust ten years later. Part of the bar was the "Ladies Ordinary" section, which served drinks to unescorted ladies without the usual social stigma of the day. During strict Victorian times it was frowned upon for single ladies to drink in public.

The hotel struggled to remain open until the 1940s when Aspen was reinvented as a ski resort. It was during this time that the hotel, especially the J-Bar, was a popular destination with the 10th Mountain Division training at nearby Camp Hale. Troops on a weekend pass would make the 82-mile trek and sleep on the lobby floor if necessary. At après ski the soldiers drank Aspen Cruds, a warm-your-soul kind of drink,

Hotel Jerome   Aspen

The J-Bar still serves Aspen Cruds, but the modern variation uses ice cream instead of milk and only three shots of bourbon. The original recipe dates back to Prohibition when bars were turned into soda fountains.

which was basically milk mixed with four shots of 90-proof bourbon.

Over the next several decades the property passed through several owners who all had intentions of restoring the Jerome to its original grandeur. The financing

Hotel Jerome   Aspen

never materialized, and demolition loomed. It wasn't until 1984 that a group of investors purchased the hotel and began a $20 million restoration effort.

The hotel was completely renovated. The old pool was replaced with a four-story addition that added 70 guest rooms, a new ballroom, and a modern fitness center complete with pool and adjoining whirlpools. A $6 million renovation in 2002 refurbished the J-Bar, guest rooms, and the main lobby.

The Hotel Jerome is finally back to the way founder Jerome B. Wheeler wanted it to be, the premier luxury hotel of the West. If he were here today, he would stand proudly in the lobby gazing at the antique crystal chandelier and magnificent marble fireplace. Perhaps this is why some souls call the Hotel Jerome their permanent resting place.

Hotel Jerome　　　　　　　　　Aspen

Little Boy Lost

A local rumor claims that in the early 1940s a little boy drowned in the old hotel pool. In the mid 80s the old pool was torn down to make way for the new north section of the hotel.

It was 1988 and Tony, the hotel's former general manger, had just started working at the Hotel Jerome. He was called to room 310, in the north section of the hotel, early one evening by a female guest who said there was a soaking wet and shivering little boy in her room.

Tony, along with a front desk employee, quickly made their way upstairs. After they entered the room, the female guest said, "I'm trying to get ready, and there's this little boy in my room. I'm in a hurry, and I think he's lost."

As the woman continued getting ready, the pair looked around the room and did not see the little boy. They checked all the usual spots--in the closet, under the bed, behind the furniture--but there was no sign of him. Then they noticed wet footprints on the carpet. The footprints were only in the center of the room and

Hotel Jerome   Aspen

did not lead anywhere like the bathroom, closet, or hallway.

"They were small like a child's," Tony said.

After a few minutes the woman thanked the pair for getting the boy out of her room. A confused Tony carefully responded, "You're welcome."

Tony and the other employee left the room. Their eyes continued to scan the hallway for the boy.

"I never saw him, nor did I ever receive any more calls from the female guest," Tony said.

The hallway outside of room 310 and throughout the third floor is where the little boy is usually seen and heard. Over the course of Tony's time at the Hotel Jerome, several overnight security guards quit after seeing the little boy.

Hotel Jerome   Aspen

The Other Woman

Another local rumor says that a chambermaid named Katie Kerrigan died in 1892 after being the victim of a prank. Kerrigan was, by all accounts, a beautiful young woman. It is said that fellow maids grew jealous of the stunning sixteen year old who was often the object of affection for many a wealthy hotel guest.

One winter evening another maid told Kerrigan that her kitten had fallen through the ice of a nearby pond. The new chambermaid rushed out onto the pond and fell through the ice. Although she didn't drown, she contracted pneumonia and died a week later.

The hotel's former general manager Tony had heard the rumor but never thought anything of it until one of his most reliable and hardest working employees quit out of the blue.

"She worked for me for 15 years and never missed a day," Tony said.

The female maid worked turndown service on the second and third floors. Turndown service only requires one person per floor as it involves turning down the covers on the bed, arranging towels, and

Hotel Jerome   Aspen

applying other finishing touches so guests can completely relax after a long day.

After 15 years on the job, the female housekeeping staffer quit because she didn't like working with the other woman.

When Tony heard this, he said, "What do you mean the other woman? She works turndown service alone!"

Tony eventually found out what had happened. When the veteran maid had finished turning down a room, she would do one last look before exiting. This was when she would discover that "the other woman" had rearranged all the towels.

"I just don't want to work with her anymore," the former maid said.

Hotel Jerome   Aspen

Turndown service is complimentary in all rooms at the Hotel Jerome, but the towels may be arranged more than once.

Hotel Jerome   **Aspen**

A Proper Hello

In June of 2004, former catering manager Jodi was working very early one morning. It was 5:30 a.m., and Jodi was by herself in the hallway on the main floor. As she walked down the long hallway that connects the original section of the hotel to the new wing, something stopped her in her tracks.

Jodi saw a ghostly male figure walk out from the entrance of Jacob's Corner restaurant. He crossed right in front of her walking from the restaurant toward the door to another eatery, the Garden Terrace. The Garden Terrace is a patio that features seasonal outdoor dining.

"He stepped directly in front of me, stopped, and tipped his hat. Then he continued walking until he disappeared through the unopened glass door of the Garden Terrace," a stunned Jodi said.

The man's face and hands were just a ghostly silhouette, his clothing was more vivid. He was wearing an old-fashioned, pale yellow tuxedo with a top hat.

Jodi knew that the man saw her.

Hotel Jerome   Aspen

"We made eye contact. He wasn't mean or anything; he just looked very peaceful and serene. I was the scared one," Jodi laughed.

After the ghostly encounter Jodi dashed back to her desk. She didn't tell anyone about the incident until several weeks later.

The hallway is just around the corner from the J-Bar. Although it connects the old section of the hotel to the new one, this area of the hallway is located within the boundaries of the original hotel.

Hotel Jerome   **Aspen**

Dog's Day

The Hotel's former general manager Tony had a loyal dog named Shadow. Tony would bring Shadow to work with him every day. He was an older dog, and his energy level matched his age.

"Every day for six years Shadow would come to work with me," Tony said.

Tony and Shadow took the same way into the hotel every day. They would pass the same ornate wood and leather chair that was just outside of Tony's office. One day Shadow ran excitedly over to the empty chair and sat down in front of it.

"He had the energy of a puppy. His ears were all perked up, and he just sat there staring at the chair as if someone was sitting there and going to pet him, but there was no one in the chair," Tony said.

Shadow never ran over to the empty chair again.

Hotel Boulderado
Boulder, Colorado

Photo courtesy of Life Exposed Photography

Boulderado.com   **800-433-4344**

History

In 1905 forward-thinking Boulder City Council Members decided that the plucky city of 8,000 could attract more people to the area by offering the comfort of a first-class hotel. Stock was offered for $100 a share, a lot of money during Victorian times. A spokesperson for the Commercial

Hotel Boulderado   Boulder

Association (a precursor to the Chamber of Commerce) said, "We have invested our money in the enterprise because it represents Boulder's greatest need. We shall be glad of returns, but shall be infinitely gladder as we secure a hotel of such beauty of proportions and architectural design that it will stand as a monument to her permanency and pride in her enterprises. Let it be the Hotel Beautiful."

    Although the inspiring quotation has lasted over 100 years, the name Hotel Beautiful didn't make it to opening day. So that no one would forget where they stayed, the words "Boulder" and "Colorado" were combined, and the Hotel Boulderado opened its doors in 1909.

    Guests were provided every comfort. Light fixtures that ran on both natural gas and electricity were installed in all 75 guest rooms. The hotel's huge coal furnace was stoked 24-hours a day to provide hot water and keep the hotel evenly heated. Telephones were also installed in most of the rooms.

    A vintage Hotel Boulderado brochure stated, "Every guest may expect the best and get it." This would explain why, over the years, famous guests have included

Hotel Boulderado   Boulder

Helen Keller, Douglas Fairbanks, Ethel Barrymore, and Louis Armstrong.

In the early 1920s a young man by the name of Hugh Mark started as an assistant to the general manager and eventually worked his way up to manager of the Hotel Boulderado. He lived at the hotel with his son in Suite 505.

Mark was, by all accounts, the heart and soul of the hotel. He believed the Hotel Boulderado should be marketed to those outside of Colorado. He worked at the hotel for 20 years and died at age 40 in the dining room of the hotel he loved.

In 1940 the Hotel Boulderado was purchased from the city of Boulder by William (Bill) Hutson Sr., as a wedding gift for his son, Bill Jr., and Bill's wife Winnie. The family had ties to the property for the next 20 years. Even Winnie's mother, Rosa May, worked for a time as the head of the housekeeping department.

Rosa lived in Room 505 until she died. This is the same room that Hugh Mark had shared with his son years earlier. Just like Hugh, Rosa also died at the hotel.

In the 1960s the Hotel Boulderado was run by the Howards. June Howard recently recalled her experiences at the hotel

Hotel Boulderado   Boulder

in an email to the hotel's website. Her first memory of the Hotel Boulderado was in 1947. She had just stepped off an all-night train ride from Kansas. Her fiancé picked her up from the train station and drove her to the most beautiful hotel she had ever seen.

"Ed [her fiancé] wanted to join me in the room. Of course I said no. It was 1947 and the old guy behind the desk watched," she said. "Little did we know that 14 years later Ed and I would be running the hotel."

In 1963 after running the hotel for a couple years, the Howards bought the property. They keep things humming until 1967 when they sold the place. The hotel was doing well financially but more renovations were needed.

However, those renovations never materialized. It was during this time when the building started to deteriorate. Finally in the 1980s the Hotel Boulderado got the attention it desperately needed, and it was restored to its original opulence.

The original cherry wood staircase still stands along with the mosaic tile floor in the lobby and dining room. Although the original lead glass ceiling was destroyed

Hotel Boulderado   Boulder

after a heavy snowfall in 1959, the current ceiling was designed to be a close match. With so many original touches still around, it's no surprise that a few souls remain here as well.

Hotel Boulderado — Boulder

Time to Shut the Door

Room 304 is a unique room as it houses one of two grandfather clocks on the premises. It's the only grandfather clock in a guest room (the other is in the lobby). All guest rooms are equipped with digital alarm clocks, so it's more of a decorative item.

It was donated after the long-term resident passed away. The rooms on the second and third floors were rented out as apartments from the 1950s to the 1970s. What is so unusual about this grandfather clock is that it never keeps the correct time.

On more than one occasion when housekeepers were vacuuming their way out of the room, the hands on the grandfather clock would start wildly swinging around for no reason. Then the hands would stop on the correct time.

"Whenever this happened, I would grab my vacuum and make a

The grandfather clock is next to the entry door of the hotel suite.

Hotel Boulderado   Boulder

quick exit," a former housekeeping staffer said.

The door that divides the parlor from the bedroom in Room 304 has also been a source of intrigue. Over the years guests would comment that the door would steadily close on its own. Even though a magnet was installed to keep the door open, it still closes on its own.

Sales & Marketing Coordinator Lynn would see the door in Room 304 close while giving history tours. Tour groups are encouraged to explore the suite first, then regroup in the parlor where the talking portion of the tour begins. It's at this point when Lynn will see the door close.

Lynn said, "It's just so strange. The door doesn't slowly squeak shut as if it was angled incorrectly, and it doesn't slam shut either. It's like someone closes it with just enough power so it shuts and latches completely."

Magnets were installed on all doors that connect two-room suites.

25

Hotel Boulderado   Boulder

The Chief Politely Declines

In the mid 80s a front desk agent was helping a guest with a late-night check in. This particular guest was an Indian chief wearing a full headdress and braids. He was escorted to room 302 at approximately 2 a.m. As soon as the bellman put the key in the door, the chief stopped him.

The chief said politely, "Please don't open this door."

The bellman obliged. The chief felt the door with his hands. After a brief pause he said he was sorry, but he couldn't go in the room.

"I don't want to disturb what's inside," the chief said.

With no other rooms available that night, management had no choice but to put him in a cab and send him to the nearby Holiday Inn.

Although the chief never entered the room, those who did have reported seeing a white shadowy figure in the mirror and smelling the scent of old-fashioned rose water perfume.

Sales & Marketing Coordinator Lynn has no explanation for this.

Hotel Boulderado   Boulder

"We don't use harsh chemical cleaners or heavy scented detergents here at the Hotel Boulderado. In fact, we are constantly complimented on our fresh smelling rooms," Lynn commented.

Lynn said another reason the hotel smells so fresh is that housekeeping opens the windows in each room for a few minutes every day.

In the fall of 2008, a radio station brought in a psychic to tour the hotel. She stopped at room 302 and said, "There's a female presence here. She is very protective of her space."

Hotel Boulderado   Boulder

Father-Son Dynamic

Just before Halloween in 2008, Sales & Marketing Coordinator Lynn was spending the night with her boyfriend in Room 505. This was the same two-room suite that longtime employee Hugh Mark and his son had shared for many years back in the 1920s and 30s.

It was early evening, and Lynn decided to take a nap. She shut the bedroom windows so that the patio noise from the bar directly below would not disturb her.

Her boyfriend was in the parlor talking on the phone with his young son. Just as Lynn was dozing off to sleep, she saw something red near the bedroom door, and then the door suddenly closed.

"I really didn't think anything of it. I assumed my boyfriend closed the door so that he would not disturb me," she said.

About an hour later she got up and walked into the parlor. She noticed that her boyfriend was wearing a blue shirt.

"Did you change your shirt?" she asked confused.

"What? No," he replied. "But I'm sorry about being so loud on the phone. I didn't

Hotel Boulderado Boulder

mean to wake you up. I saw you in your white nightie shutting the door."

"You didn't wake me, but I didn't shut the door. You did. And you had a red shirt on," Lynn said confused. "And I'm not wearing a white nightie."

They both agreed that neither one of them had closed the door. He saw a lady in a white dress near the door, and Lynn saw someone wearing red. Perhaps whoever closed the door wanted to ensure that the phone conversation between father and son would continue in private.

The door is located just inches from the bed where Lynn was sleeping. Photo courtesy of Life Exposed Photography.

Hotel Boulderado   Boulder

I Didn't Just See That

    In winter of 2009, Event Set Up Manager Ben was working in his office on the second floor when he saw a dark figure move across the doorway. He also heard the hangers that line the wall rustle as if someone was brushing by them.

    The hangers, which are used for table linen storage, are situated on the opposite side of the room from where Ben's desk is located. Someone moving in that direction would exit Ben's office and enter a storage room. Although the storage room has a window and a door, it was winter, and they were both closed.

    "I didn't just see that," Ben said out loud, half joking.

    Someone replied, "Yes, you did!"

    At this point Ben was startled. He knew there was an intruder in the room, and he was prepared for a fight. He pretended to leave his office and loudly shut his office door. Then he quietly grabbed a metal pipe and snuck over to the storage room.

    Once inside he quickly flicked on the light and yelled, "You're not supposed to be in here!"

Hotel Boulderado   Boulder

Much to Ben's surprise, the storage room was empty, and the door and window were both closed. He opened the door and quickly stepped into the hallway, which was also empty.

The hanging table linens were jostled as the mysterious figure moved toward the storage room door in the background.

Hotel Boulderado — Boulder

Mezzanine Mystery Man

Over the years there have been reports of sneezing and coughing on the second floor mezzanine when no one is in the area. In April of 2010, Event Set Up Manager Ben was stacking chairs one afternoon when he saw a tall, older man in a brown suit standing near him.

When Ben turned to ask the man if he could be of assistance, the man was gone. In fact, Ben was completely alone. The only other item nearby was a vacuum cleaner.

"I didn't see a vacuum cleaner. I saw a man, and that man was definitely taller than the vacuum cleaner," Ben stated.

Ben saw the man in the brown suit standing near the love seat.

Hotel Boulderado   Boulder

A Lady Always Flushes Twice

In winter of 2010, a big, burly male guest arrived at the front desk to check out at 5 a.m. He was staying in room 511, and appeared extremely nervous.

When the front desk clerk asked the guest about his stay, the man said he was woken at 3 a.m. by a "lady in white."

"I woke up and saw this white figure standing over my bed. It looked like a female," the man said.

She went into the bathroom, flushed the toilet twice, then disappeared.

"I've never seen anything like it," the man said with a shaky voice.

Guests staying in room 511 have also heard footsteps when no one is there.

Historic Brown Hotel & Restaurant
Breckenridge, Colorado

Historicbrown.com   (970) 453-0084

History

The Historic Brown was built in the mid-1800s as a private residence. By the 1880s the building was a school operated by Union Captain George L. Ryan and his wife. By the 1900s it was a high-end hotel run by owners Tom and Maude Brown, for whom the property was eventually named.

Historic Brown Breckenridge

During the early 1900s the mining slump brought Breckenridge's population from 5,000 to a mere 250. The Brown managed to make due probably because, as one story suggests, the property housed the only bathtub in Summit county.

Local legend states that around the turn of the century, a madam named Ms. Whitney wanted to expand her business. She planned to move into the Brown and operate it as a high-end brothel. To help facilitate the process, she began a romance with the hotel's owner. Shortly after the couple's engagement Ms. Whitney's fiancé found out about her plans and shot her in the upstairs bedroom.

Over the years the property went through a series of owners. Some had good hearts and tried their best to make an honest profit. However, one previous owner in particular made irrational remodeling decisions and was, by all accounts, too drunk to run a business.

In the 1980s the Cavanaughs bought the property, renovated it, and operated it as a high-end restaurant. The fine dining continued until tourists started renting condos with kitchens, and the need for a nice restaurant dwindled.

Historic Brown　　　　Breckenridge

　　　Michael Cavanaugh still runs the Historic Brown Hotel and Restaurant. Cajun and Mexican food is complimentary with the purchase of a beverage, and the locals love it, especially the Brown's famous stuffed shrimp. Perhaps this is why some hungry souls never leave.

Historic Brown   **Breckenridge**

Bam, Bam, Bam, Bam

It was back in the fall of 1985 when Nanci, the current owner's ex-wife, was renovating and running the Historic Brown with Michael. It was late at night, between 2 and 3 a.m., when Nanci decided she was too tired to wait for her husband to take her home. At the time they lived in a house on the outskirts of Breckenridge.

    Nanci headed upstairs from the restaurant to sleep in the bedroom. She assumed Michael would follow her upstairs when he was finished closing up. He did not. Instead he left and drove home.

    Unable to sleep, Nanci lay awake waiting for her husband when she heard the hangers in the bedroom closet rustle as if someone was moving around in there.

    Just then the bedroom door flew open, hit the wall, and slammed shut. And then again it opened, hit the wall, and slammed shut. This happened four times in a row.

    She thought it was Michael outside the bedroom door trying to scare her. So she got up and made her way out of the room.

Historic Brown Breckenridge

Annoyed, she yelled, "Michael!"

As she stood at the top of the dimly lit stairway, she could feel a dark presence standing right in front of her. She felt incredibly threatened.

"I was absolutely terrified," she said. "It was right near my face. I couldn't see anything, but it's the same feeling you get when a stranger is standing way too close to you."

Nanci bolted downstairs. She could feel the presence chasing her all the way down the stairs. She ran out onto the porch. She stood there in her stocking feet not sure what to do.

"This was before cell phones, and I wasn't going back inside. I knew that the police would think I was crazy, but I didn't care. I was scared," she said.

With snow on the ground she ran in her socks several blocks to the police station. She was able to call Michael, who had been at home for about 20 minutes, and got a ride home.

There was no evidence of an intruder or of Michael trying to scare her, but Nanci never slept at the Historic Brown again.

Historic Brown   Breckenridge

The top of the stairs is just outside the old bedroom where Nanci was trying to sleep.

Historic Brown — Breckenridge

3 Hot Spots, 1 Creepy Photo

Former bartender Bryan worked at the Historic Brown from 2008 to 2010. During his time at the Brown, there were three "hot spots" that always seemed to have unexplained happenings: the kitchen, the basement, and the women's restroom. In ghost hunting circles hot spot refers to a particular area with unusually high occurrences of paranormal activity.

As a bartender Bryan also helped close the kitchen at night. After washing the pots and pans, Bryan would grab them to put them away. He would lean into the sink and with his elbow turn off the water. Several times upon returning to the sink, he would find the water on full blast.

"It wasn't a trickle like I didn't turn it off all the way. It would be gushing out of the faucet even stronger than when I was washing dishes," Bryan said.

The basement, specifically the stockroom, also had an ongoing unexplained event. Out of nowhere the smell of ladies' perfume would overwhelm the room even when no women were in the building.

"It was a very distinct smell. It was the type of perfume that you just don't

Historic Brown Breckenridge

smell anymore, something that your grandmother or great-grandmother may have worn. I've never smelled it before or since," Bryan said. "But I'd recognize it if I smelled it again."

The women's bathroom was another spot that was a cause of concern, not because of the smell or faucets with minds of their own, but because it had a feeling of dread. Many patrons would come out of the bathroom with an uneasy feeling, vowing to never use it again.

Bryan's girlfriend Mary hated using that bathroom and usually took a friend with her when she did. It wasn't until her friend Christine went into the bathroom with her and shouted, "Leave Mary alone!" that the uneasy feeling ceased.

"After that, Mary had no problem using the ladies' room alone," Bryan said.

Even after all these experiences Bryan wasn't scared. He thinks it's all interesting and a little weird.

Perhaps the most interesting thing that Bryan experienced was a photograph he took one night while waiting for his first customers to arrive.

"I was bored and messing around with my camera phone. Sitting on the

Historic Brown Breckenridge

couch I took a picture in negative, which means the colors are reversed [anything black appears white, and vice versa] of the fire in the fireplace," Bryan said.

Although nothing unusual appeared in the fire when Bryan took the picture, the photo shows what appears to be a human torso with the profile of an animal skull in the fire.

Hotel St. Nicholas
Cripple Creek, Colorado

Hotelstnicholas.com   888-786-4257

History

In 1894 Sister Mary Claver Coleman was sent to Cripple Creek, CO, by the Sisters of Mercy to establish the town's first general hospital. The Sisters of Mercy is a worldwide Catholic organization that ministers to the sick and poor. The group is well known throughout Colorado for establishing hospitals in mining towns.

Hotel St. Nicholas   Cripple Creek

The Sisters' original hospital was located a block away from the current Hotel St. Nicholas. In April of 1896, a massive fire destroyed most of Cripple Creek. While the Sisters were busy evacuating patients, a member of an anti-Catholic society attempted to destroy the building by placing dynamite in the stove. To the man's misfortune, it exploded prematurely. Although the hospital sustained very little damage, the man's leg was blown off.

Due to the kindhearted and forgiving nature of the Sisters, the man was evacuated along with the patients. He was cared for so compassionately by the Sisters that the man repented and expressed deep remorse for what he had done. His shoe, which landed in a tea kettle after the explosion, was kept by the Sisters as a memento.

Although the hospital survived the Cripple Creek fire and the attempted terrorist attack, the Sisters decided they needed a safer and more up-to-date structure. Completed in 1898 for $12,000, the current building was dubbed the St. Nicholas Hospital. Named for and dedicated by then Colorado Bishop Nicholas Matz, it was a thoroughly modern hospital.

Hotel St. Nicholas   Cripple Creek

It featured electric lights, steam heat, hot and cold running water, and an operating room.

The Sisters ran the hospital until 1924 when the hospital was purchased by a series of doctors. By this time the mines were closing, and the town's population was shrinking. The hospital finally closed in 1972, and the facility was used as a boarding house and even stood vacant for a while.

The current owner, Susan Adelbush, purchased the property in 1995 and completely refurbished it into a historic hotel. Although updated with all modern amenities, the building still has original touches and, perhaps, even a few of its original inhabitants.

Hotel St. Nicholas   Cripple Creek

Petey

On the main floor of the Hotel St. Nicholas is a popular watering hole called the Boiler Room. It's a small but charming joint frequented by visitors and locals. Its decor features artifacts from the hotel's and Cripple Creek's past.

Over the years bartenders and patrons alike have noticed that on random occasions bottles and glasses will fly off the bar and land on the floor. What is so strange is that these items don't just tumble over the side because someone has put them too close to the edge. They fly out from the bar at high speed, travel two or three feet horizontally in the air, then drop to the floor.

Former bartender Amy thinks "Petey" is responsible for these pranks. "I named him Petey because his pranks seemed so mischievous," she said. Petey also loves to hide cigarettes and play with the old-fashioned cash register.

Amy recalled an incident after the hotel first opened in the late 1990s. It was just her and one customer in the bar when a bottle of Crown Royal Special Reserve sitting on the windowsill exploded into

Hotel St. Nicholas   Cripple Creek

pieces like someone was using it as target practice. At first Amy and the bar patron thought a stone kicked up from a passing car outside had somehow come through the window and broken the bottle. When they checked the window, there was no sign of an entry point. "My first thought was 'Jeez, Petey, you couldn't break the bottle of Barcardi? Why did it have to be the $50 bottle of Crown Royal?'" Amy laughed.

Petey doesn't limit himself to adult beverages either. Not long after the Crown Royal incident Amy had poured herself a protein shake. She set the shake on the bar and went to clean out the blender. She and three customers watched as her protein shake was levitated up in the air, flipped over three times without spilling, and then dropped to the floor with a splat.

"Great! Another Petey mess for me to clean up," Amy said.

Hotel St. Nicholas   Cripple Creek

Petey plays pranks in the bar but has never been seen. There have also been reports of children running and playing in the hallways late at night when no children are staying at the hotel.

Hotel St. Nicholas   Cripple Creek

The Quiet Observer

It was winter of 2003, and the owner Susan was working in the office one afternoon. She had her back to the check-in counter when she sensed that someone had walked into the lobby.

"Although I didn't hear anyone come in, I just knew someone was there," Susan said.

When she turned around she saw a thick, gray figure with a top hat sitting on the stool near the computer. He was just quietly sitting there with his legs crossed. Although he didn't move, "I could tell he had just sat down because as soon as I looked at him, his long coat fell open near the bottom as if he had just sat down and crossed his legs," Susan said.

He didn't say or do anything; he was just watching her. "I didn't get any sense that he was trying to hurt or scare me. He just seemed curious and interested in what I was doing," Susan said.

Even though Susan didn't feel threatened, common sense prevailed, and "I ran out of the room just in case!" Susan joked.

Hotel St. Nicholas   Cripple Creek

The gray figure was sitting on a stool in the office just on the other side of the check-in desk. By the time Susan came back into the office, the figure was gone.

Hotel St. Nicholas   **Cripple Creek**

The Angelic Light

In March of 2001, Southwest Ghost Hunters Association took pictures of different locations around the property while doing an investigation. A picture taken in Room 6 showed what appeared to be a bright light on the wall above the bed. The light was long and lean, shaped like a nun wearing a habit (see below).

This photo is courtesy of the Southwest Ghost Hunters Association. For more photos of the Hotel St. Nicholas, paranormal investigation results, or more details, go to SGHA.net.

The hotel was run by the Sisters of Mercy until 1924, so the owner was a little relieved that they were still around. "It was

Hotel St. Nicholas   Cripple Creek

rather comforting to hear," Susan said. "Other than that I didn't think much about it until a few years later."

About 5 years later a guest staying in Room 6 woke in the middle of the night because of the bright light on the wall above his bed. Since there were no lights on in his room, he figured it was some type of reflection. He touched the light to try to create a shadow on it so that he could see where it was coming from. No matter where he touched it or from what angle, he just couldn't make a shadow appear on the light.

As the man stood back from the bed, he saw a rough outline of a nun with eyes, nose, and a mouth. "It lasted 15-20 minutes; then it was gone," the man said.

The next morning the man relayed the story to Susan, who asked him if he had seen the picture that the ghost hunters had taken years before. He had not seen the photo but confirmed he saw the same thing. "He seemed relieved that someone else had seen it too," Susan said.

Hotel St. Nicholas   Cripple Creek

This photo of Room 6 was taken in May 2010. This is the same room, but the furniture has been rearranged.

Lumber Baron Inn
Denver, Colorado

Lumberbaron.com   (303) 477-8205

History

In 1890 John Mouat built the mansion on West 37th Avenue and Bryant as a private residence for his wife and five children. Mouat was a Scottish immigrant turned lumber baron whose company, Mouat Lumber, constructed more than 200 buildings in Denver. He saved the best for himself and his family.

Lumber Baron Inn   Denver

The 8,500-square-foot structure was the grandest house in the Potter Highlands neighborhood. Each room featured a different type of wood. The third floor was used to host lavish parties. It boasted a high ceiling and beautiful maple floor.

In 1904 the building housed the Denver Business University. By 1909 the university had left, and the structure began a 70-year connection to three generations of the Fowler family.

The family began taking in boarders in the 1920s. James Fowler took over the property in the late 1940s and made renovations, like adding bathrooms to most of the bedrooms. He was a well-known Denver Socialist.

In October of 1970, 17-year-old tenant Cara Knoche was brutally raped and strangled to death. Minutes later her friend, 18-year-old Marianne Weaver, stumbled upon the horrible scene and was fatally shot. The double homicide remains a Denver cold case.

By the 1980s the once magnificent mansion was nothing more than a run-down tenement building. The property really hit rock bottom when it was bought by an alleged slumlord who never actually

Lumber Baron Inn   Denver

resided in the building. According to a local rumor, a gang-affiliated renter lost his leg in an ax fight in the main living room in 1989. A year later the city finally condemned the place.

In 1991 Walter Keller bought the property and began the long and expensive remodeling effort to restore the building to its original grandeur. Today the Lumber Baron Inn and Gardens is elegantly restored and serves as one of Denver's most beautiful examples of Queen Anne Architecture. It hosts weddings, murder mystery weekends, and overnight guests.

Since the Lumber Baron Inn has opened, workers, guests, and visitors have reported strange occurrences, ghost sightings, and disembodied voices. With such a turbulent past, it's not surprising that the Lumber Baron Inn has more to offer than your typical wedding venue.

Lumber Baron Inn   Denver

Stares from the Staircase

Since the building has reopened there is one spirit who isn't afraid of being seen. She has been seen on random occasions throughout the years but always in the same spot, the landing of the grand staircase in the main entryway.

The owner Walter said, "I'll be walking through the main floor and get this eerie sense that I'm being watched."

Then he will look up on the grand staircase and see a woman, with her arms folded across her chest staring at him. Dressed in Victorian garb with her dark hair pulled tightly back in a bun, she doesn't move or say anything.

"She's very stern looking with her lips pressed tightly together. It doesn't scare me, but she certainly doesn't look very happy," Walter said.

Walter thinks she was a faculty member from the Denver Business University. The building housed the school from 1904 to 1909.

Lumber Baron Inn   Denver

The woman on the staircase wore a long black skirt and a frilly white blouse with a high collar.

Lumber Baron Inn   **Denver**

Room within a Room

In the early 1990s, shortly after owner Walter moved in, a police officer stopped by and wanted to talk to him. The officer was investigating a cold case from a few years earlier involving the property and wanted to know if Walter had any additional information.

Walter did not but was curious to know more about the cold case. The policewoman said it was a missing person's case that had a connection to the neighborhood, but beyond that there were no leads whatsoever. A psychic was consulted to drive around the area with the officer to see if she could sense anything.

When they passed the former Mouat Mansion at West 37th and Byrant, the psychic said, "It's this house. We need to go in here."

At the time the property was a run-down apartment building. The main door was unlocked so the pair were able to get inside without issue. After they walked up to the third floor, the psychic reported feeling weak but managed to keep going when they found a back staircase. They used it to get down to the basement.

Lumber Baron Inn   Denver

    Once in the basement they found a stonewalled room containing the boiler and laundry machines. The psychic had a strong sense that they were in the right place. The psychic stayed in that room for thirty minutes and eventually started muttering, "Room within a room, room within a room."

    The officer didn't know what to think, there weren't any other rooms they could check. Figuring it was just another dead end and with her shift ending, she told the psychic they had to leave.

    Walter was stunned. He knew nothing of this story. The police officer eventually left, but Walter "got to thinking about it" and decided to do some investigating of his own.

    He went to the basement near where the old boiler was and started looking around. He noticed that behind some shelving there seemed to be no support wall in one area. He took down the shelves and shined his flashlight into the dark space. He saw another room--a room within a room. It was a long, narrow space with a dirt floor and cobwebs.

Lumber Baron Inn   Denver

Walter gathered his courage (and a couple of friends) and entered what seemed to be a 20- to 30-foot-long tunnel behind the basement wall. A few feet inside he shined his flashlight behind him and saw that dirt had been dug out from underneath the basement floor. Retracing his steps, he noticed that he was walking over what appeared to be a six-foot long mound in the tunnel floor. It looked as if something were buried there using dirt from underneath the basement.

Walter also found a broken shovel and some dirty old clothes lying under the basement floor. Further investigation of the tunnel proved it led to a manhole cover on the street. Later research showed this tunnel was actually an old coal chute, not uncommon during Victorian times.

Walter and his friends had to find out what was underneath the dirt. They spent most of the night removing dirt until they dug all the way down to the bedrock. They found nothing.

Walter and his friends were disappointed. "That doesn't mean that something, or someone, wasn't buried there at one time and later moved," Walter said.

Lumber Baron Inn   Denver

Every year, near Halloween, the Lumber Baron Inn hosts a paranormal event where the latest details on the missing person's case, as well as other stories involving the property, are revealed. For more information on upcoming events, visit lumberbaron.com.

The old coal chute tunnel still connects the Lumber Baron Inn with the sidewalk out front. Walter was in contact with the police regarding the room within a room. So far, the police are guarding the details.

Lumber Baron Inn   **Denver**

A Sad Anniversary

On October 13, 2000, exactly 30 years after the unsolved murders of Cara Knoche and Marianne Weaver (see Lumber Baron Inn History, page 57), a well-known paranormal author, Dee Chandler, was brought in to do a walkthrough of the property. A paranormal investigative team accompanied her to record any findings. An enthusiastic tour group was also there to witness the events of the evening.

This was a unique night. Not only was it the 30-year anniversary of the double homicide, but it was also a Friday (Friday the 13th), and it was a full moon. "If something was going to happen, this was going to be the night," Walter, the owner, said.

According to an October 19, 2003, *Denver Post* article, Chandler said, "Everybody experienced something that night, and they all reported it individually."

The group as a whole witnessed the refrigerator shifting back and forth. Complete details of the investigation can be found in Chandler's book Ghost *Hunter: A Guide To Ghost Photography and Field Investigations*, available at Amazon.com.

Lumber Baron Inn   Denver

The following photographs were taken during the paranormal investigation.

The owner Walter has no explanation as to why a cat appears on the windowsill in this picture. He does not own any cats. Photo courtesy of Dee Chandler.

The reflection in the lower right hand corner of the mirror resembles murder victim Marianne Weaver. Mirror photo courtesy of Dee Chandler.

Lumber Baron Inn   **Denver**

Justice for Cara & Marianne

According to newspaper reports, the case has been reopened many times only to have the trail grow cold. The current owner Walter has leads come in from time to time and has been in contact with the police. If you have any information regarding the events of October 13, 1970, at 2555 West 37th Ave in Denver, contact Denver Crime Stoppers at (720) 913-7867 or go to metro-denvercrimestoppers.com.

Someone out there knows something. Maybe you're the key that will help bring justice to two grieving families. "I hope justice can be served," Walter said. "It could make a difference with the energies in the house."

Lumber Baron Inn — Denver

The Accidental EVP

Electronic Voice Phenomenon (EVP) in paranormal circles refers to the audio recording of disembodied voices or sounds. When conducting research for my books, I always record my interviews not because I'm trying to capture an EVP but because I would rather not rely on my handwritten notes, or worse, my memory, for all the details of a story.

My education in journalism has trained me to always check facts (thanks, Michigan State University). My practical experience has taught me to record everything to save time, energy, and most importantly, to cover my butt (thanks, former jobs).

When writing the Lumber Baron Inn chapter for this book, I was playing back my interview with owner Walter Keller. Several minutes into the interview I heard what sounded like a person or perhaps a cat screaming twice about five seconds apart. I don't remember this noise, or any other unusual noises, during our conversation, and neither of us acknowledges it on the recording.

Lumber Baron Inn   Denver

    What makes this accidental EVP really interesting is that it occurs during Walter's explanation of the paranormal investigation results from a few years earlier (see "A Sad Anniversary," page 66). He was showing me one of the pictures taken during the investigation of a cat on a windowsill (see top photo on page 67). Walter does not own any cats.

    I have loaded the EVP audio file to my fan page on Facebook. To hear it for yourself, become a fan of one of my books: *Michigan's Most Haunted: A Ghostly Guide the Great Lakes State,* or *Colorado's Most Haunted: A Ghostly Guide to the Rocky Mountain State.*

Redstone Inn
Redstone, Colorado

Redstoneinn.com   (970) 963-2526

History

In 1892 coal baron John Cleveland Osgood merged his successful coal business with an iron and steel company in Pueblo to form the Colorado Fuel and Iron Company. The merger spurred the construction of the Crystal River Railroad to transport the coal to the main railroad lines in Carbondale and finally to the steel mills in Pueblo.

Redstone Inn   Redstone

The Redstone Inn and surrounding structures were originally built as housing for miners and their families. Osgood didn't build low-end bunkhouses, which were common in mining towns; instead he constructed state-of-the-art facilities.

As part of a social and industrial experiment, Osgood wanted to improve the living conditions for his employees. Eighty-four Swiss-chalet style homes were built for miners with families, along with 20 elegant rooms in the main building for bachelors. All featured indoor plumbing and electricity. Also on the property was a clubhouse with a theater and library.

Osgood's private residence, the lavish Cleveholm Manor, was a 42-room Tudor-style home complete with servants quarters, guard and carriage houses. The good times didn't last, and Osgood lost most of his company in a bitter stock war in 1909. He managed to hold on to his beloved Redstone Inn, but left the area and disappeared from public view for 16 years.

Osgood returned in 1925 with his third wife Lucille. The pair renovated the property and turned it into the historic

Redstone Inn   Redstone

Redstone Inn. A year later Osgood died and left Lucille his entire estate.

Lucille ran the resort until 1941, but by then the population of Redstone had dwindled to just 14 residents. The property sat vacant for many years and fell into disrepair.

It wasn't until 1989 when John F. Gilmore purchased the property that the Redstone Inn finally got the attention it deserved. After a huge remodeling effort the Redstone Inn once again shined with its original glory.

Six of the 84 Swiss-style cottages still remain on the property. They now serve as seasonal shops in Redstone Village just a few steps away from the Redstone Inn. In fact, the area looks much the same as it did during Osgood's time. Maybe that's why he and a few other souls still reside at the Redstone Inn.

Redstone Inn

A Beer for Spirits

Back in the early 1990s Redstone Inn bar employees thought they had a prankster working on staff. After closing the bar at night, the last employee to leave would turn off the lights and lock the door. The next morning staff would arrive to find bar stools turned over and broken bottles on the floor.

At first the staff started blaming each other. After they determined that none of them were responsible for the mayhem, they turned to a different explanation, an unhappy spirit. The group figured that if a spirit were hanging around in a bar, maybe it wanted a drink.

So every night after closing, someone would leave an opened bottle of beer on the corner of the bar. Although the bottle of beer would still be full in the morning, never again was there overturned bar stools or broken glass to clean up.

Redstone Inn   Redstone

The nightly ritual continued until a Ute Indian Chief visited the Redstone Inn. He heard the story and decided to perform a ritual asking the spirit to leave. It worked. Beers were no longer left overnight, and the bar has been in working order every morning since.

The Lone Soldier

In the winter of 2007, longtime Redstone Inn employee Katie was working the night shift alone. It was about 2 a.m., and she had just returned from doing security rounds. As she stepped back into the lobby, something caught her attention.

She saw a male soldier just standing there in the lobby. He was wearing a Civil War era uniform with a cap. This wasn't a gray figure or a shadow. He looked real. Katie could see blonde hair sticking out of his hat. He didn't move and had an empty expression on his face.

"He didn't acknowledge me at all. He just stared right through me like I wasn't there," Katie said.

After a few moments he vanished as if someone had switched off a light.

Katie never felt threatened by the lone soldier in the lobby.

Night Whispers

In the winter of 2005, a former guest called the Redstone Inn regarding her stay a couple of months earlier. She didn't call to complain but instead to relay a remarkable experience she couldn't stop thinking about.

The guest had stayed in the Osgood Suite with her husband. She said she was awakened in the middle of the night because someone was whispering in her ear. At first she thought it was her husband, but when she turned to see what he wanted, he was sound asleep.

The first time it happened she dismissed it as maybe her husband was talking in his sleep although he wasn't prone to doing so. She eventually fell back asleep and was awakened again two more times that same night. Each time she thought it was her husband, but he was still sleeping quietly beside her.

The former guest said, "I know someone was whispering in my ear. I could feel their breath on my ear. I can't stop dreaming about it, so I had to call and tell you."

Redstone Inn — Redstone

Although the former guest couldn't understand anything the night whisperer said, she'll never forget the experience.

Redstone Inn

Redstone

Third Floor Fiesta

It was the middle of winter 2007, and the only guests at the Redstone Inn were a couple staying on the second floor. The morning after the couple's first night at the hotel, they asked the front desk attendant, "Who's on the third floor having a party?"

A confused desk clerk said, "Party? You heard a party?"

"Oh yes," the couple said. "Loud music, people talking and laughing. I could even hear the children. They were playing with their bouncy balls right outside our door."

The desk clerk replied carefully, "But you're the only guests here right now. And, except for night security and myself, there were no other people in the building last night."

The employee later said, "I don't think they believed me. But they never complained about the noise again during their stay."

Redstone Inn   Redstone

The third floor has six guest rooms, all of which were empty that night.

Redstone Castle
Redstone, Colorado

Redstonecastle.us   (970) 963-9656

History

Redstone Castle was originally built as a private residence for coal baron and Redstone Inn owner John Cleveland Osgood. The lavish Cleveholm Manor, as it was called, featured 42 rooms complete with servants quarters, guard and carriage houses. It is located just down the road from the Redstone Inn.

Redstone Castle   Redstone

Although Osgood originally built the manor for his first wife, it was his second wife, Swedish Countess Alma Regina Shelgrem, who is credited for much of the castle's charm. Alma was known as "Lady Bountiful" by the residents of Redstone for her generosity.

The Redstone Castle interior features a peep window that allowed Lady Bountiful to view her guests as they arrived in the great room downstairs. This way she could change clothes to fit in with whatever style her female guests were sporting.

The walls of the castle are filled with black-and-white images of Osgood throughout the years, along with his three wives. He was a ruthless and eccentric businessman who never dined with more than eight guests and only at a round dinner table.

Although Osgood lost most of his fortune in a bitter stock war, he managed to hold on to the Cleveholm and died in residence in 1926. His third wife, Lucille, was sole inheritor of his estate. She lived at Cleveholm Manor until 1944.

Over the next 40 years the property went through several owners, names, and incarnations. It was a lodge, a resort, and

Redstone Castle

a bed and breakfast. By the 1990s the Redstone Castle had been in and out of foreclosure several times.

It was seized by the IRS in 2003 as part of a fraud scheme investigation. Its ownership was undecided until a March 2005 auction when part-time Aspenite Ralli Dimitrius paid $4 million and become the owner of the historic property.

In 2006 the movie *The Prestige*, starring Michael Caine, Hugh Jackman, Christian Bale, and Scarlett Johansson, was filmed at Redstone Castle.

As of 2011 the castle is undergoing major renovations in preparation for the highly anticipated opening of the Redstone Castle Resort & Spa. The plan is to operate a luxury resort, including a full-service spa, pool, conservatory, fine dining room, and upscale bar.

Until then, tours are available year round. Tour-goers are encouraged to take photographs and discover why some souls have checked into the Redstone Castle and never checked out.

Redstone Castle

Blast from the Past

In the fall of 2001, longtime employee Sue was working at the Redstone Castle as the restaurant manager. It was early evening, and the dinner rush had just started.

Sue exited the dining room and walked into the great room, which also was the waiting area, when she noticed a woman sitting on the couch. The woman was alone with her back to Sue.

"What struck me about her was her hairstyle. She wore her hair in an old-fashioned beehive. It was all teased up on the top of her head like Marge Simpson. That's not something you see every day," Sue said.

Sue made a mental note that there was a customer waiting but had to make a quick trip down the hall to the kitchen. Upon her return just seconds later, the woman was gone. The room was empty.

Sue originally thought the woman had been seated, but when she checked the dining room, she did not see her. Sue asked other staff members if anyone had seen a woman with the beehive hairstyle. No one had.

Redstone Castle   Redstone

"No one has seen a woman with a beehive since the early 1970s," Sue joked.

The woman with the beehive had light-colored hair and sat on the couch in the foreground. The woman was never seen again.

Redstone Castle — Redstone

Cigar, Cigar, Wherever You Are

Although smoking is banned inside most Colorado buildings, the smell of cigar smoke lingers on at the Redstone Castle. This isn't because a few rebels are sneaking a puff.

Some believe John Cleveland Osgood, the original owner of Redstone properties, is back visiting his beloved home. In fact, enjoying a fine cigar was one of his favorite ways to end a day.

"I have smelled cigar smoke in all of the rooms throughout the castle grounds, even in winter when the windows are closed," said longtime employee Sue.

Sue is not the only one to notice. Other employees and guests have asked, "Is that cigar smoke?"

Evidence of anyone smoking has never been found. There are no cigar butts or ashtrays.

Redstone Castle   Redstone

Original owner John Cleveland Osgood loved to smoke cigars on his covered porch near his bedroom.

The Grand Imperial Hotel
Silverton, Colorado

Grandimperialhotel.com   800-341-3340

History

The town of Silverton, CO, was established in 1874 by miners seeking their fortunes in the gold and silver mines. Eight years later ground was broken on what would eventually become the Grand Imperial Hotel. Although the original plans did not include a hotel, when the large brick building on Greene Street finally

Grand Imperial Hotel   Silverton

opened in 1883 it included two clothing stores, two hardware stores and, on the third floor, a hotel.

That same year the new railroad brought an influx of gamblers, prostitutes, and con men. City ordinances against such lewd actions levied fines on perpetrators, which ironically provided a major source of income for the growing city. In fact, this revenue was so steady that it kept the town going without imposing property taxes on its citizens.

To keep the debauchery under control, an imaginary line was drawn down Greene Street dividing the brothels and gambling houses from the more reputable establishments. Although the building was not located on the "liquor" side of Greene Street, the businesses there were constantly being burglarized, robbed, and harassed. From 1885 to 1929, the hotel and associated saloons had countless robberies and brawls that usually ended with gunfire and the death of the perpetrators and/or innocent bystanders.

In the 1920s the building was bought by Henry Frecker, who was an odd fellow. Although a successful miner, he remained

Grand Imperial Hotel   Silverton

This boarded up storage area is all that remains of an old tunnel that ran beneath Greene Street. It was used by pedestrians who wanted to access the brothels and gambling houses across the street without being seen.

frugal and kept to himself. Nonetheless, his building was going through many positive changes. The old saloon became the American Cafe, and the hotel was leased to Rosa Stewart.

Grand Imperial Hotel   Silverton

    The American Cafe was an extremely popular restaurant with everyone in town. It was one of the few places that served both the good, upstanding citizens and the prostitutes working in the bordellos across the street. Laws restricted the movement of the "working girls" by allowing them only two hours a day to pick up their mail, do their shopping, and have dinner at the American Cafe. Even a portion of the restaurant was screened off to shelter the "good" people in town from the riffraff.
    After a year of renovations, Rosa Stewart reopened the hotel in 1926. By then Prohibition was in full swing, and Silverton, along with most of the country, was dry. Like prostitution and gambling, Silverton tolerated alcohol, and many of the old saloons still housed illegal distilleries in their basements.
    In 1928 Rosa was arrested for possessing "Bootleg Hootch." No one was surprised as she had a reputation for bending the law from time to time. Although one of her guests admitted to hiding the moonshine, she was found guilty and ordered to pay $150.

Grand Imperial Hotel   Silverton

A year later hotel guest John Zink, for reasons known only to him, became angry with Rosa and starting shooting at her. He must have been a bad shot as she survived with only minor flesh wounds. Minutes later John committed suicide in the hotel office on the second floor.

In the mid 1930s, Rosa left, and Henry Frecker, the owner of the building, took over the management of the hotel until his death in 1944. Known for being "so cheap he squeaks," he seldom kept the furnace hot enough to heat the building properly, and the rooms were always cold.

An old story from Don Stott's 1974 book, *Where the Mountains Meet the Sky*, tells of a man who died of hypothermia on Ophir Pass (in the mountains). When the sheriff came into the lobby of the hotel and told a small crowd that a man had frozen to death, someone jokingly asked, "What room was he in?"

After Henry's death the hotel passed to one of his relatives, Edna Frecker. She was responsible for cleaning up Silverton and ridding the town of gambling and prostitutes. Edna ran the hotel until 1950 when she sold out to Winfield Morten, a rich Texan.

Grand Imperial Hotel   Silverton

According to Allan Bird's 1995 book, *The Grand Imperial Hotel Story,* Winfield had dreams of attracting other wealthy Texans. He believed that by not allowing locals to patronize his new hotel, his rich friends would feel more comfortable. He got his wish, no locals ever stepped foot in his hotel, but neither did his wealthy friends. He was forced into bankruptcy in 1963.

In 1971 Don and Dorothy Stott made their annual trip to Silverton and learned that the building was scheduled for demolition. Against the advice of their accountants, they sold their home and profitable Philadelphia business to join the hotel industry. After doing most of the renovations themselves and suffering significant financial losses for the first two years, things turned around.

Silverton was finally being discovered as one of the last remaining frontier mining towns of the west. The hotel's current owners, the Foster family, purchased the property in 1993 and continue to improve upon its charm, while never forgetting its colorful past. In fact, some guests of the Grand Imperial Hotel still roam the halls.

Grand Imperial Hotel   Silverton

The Sad Story of Luigi Regalia

Although the hotel's early years were marked by bloodshed and corruption, nothing was as sad as the story of Luigi Regalia. Born in Pozzolo, Italy, in 1848, he came to America in 1879. He relocated to Silverton in 1881 and had many friends, but he longed for the girl he left behind in Italy.

Luigi attempted to raise money to bring her over from Italy, but it was not to be, and he spiraled into a depression. In room 28 at 10:30 on a November night in 1890, he picked up a Smith & Wesson revolver and shot himself in the head.

According to Dan, the hotel's current manager, room 28 no longer exists as the hotel's rooms have been renumbered starting at 201. His best guess is that old room 28 is the current room 314. However, this doesn't seem to matter because Luigi doesn't confine himself to only one room. Dan has seen him throughout the hotel.

Since 1992 Dan regularly sees Luigi in the reflection of the glass picture frames that hang in the hallways. He appears as a shadowy figure with his distinctive derby hat.

Grand Imperial Hotel   Silverton

"I just know it's him," Dan stated calmly. "He's not trying to hurt anyone. He just wants me to know he's still here."

A couple times a month Dan sees Luigi's reflection following him down the hallways.

"He plays pranks, too," explained Dan. "There's only two months out of the year when we are completely closed November and April. I'm the last person to leave and the first person to arrive. And three or four times now I've come in to find all the furniture stacked on top of each other and pushed to the center of the dining room. I never hear it move. I never see it move."

Grand Imperial Hotel   Silverton

The heavy wood furniture would require several people to move without scraping the floor.

Grand Imperial Hotel   Silverton

Four Ghosts and a Spider

Dan has worked for the Grand Imperial since 1988, but it wasn't until 1992 that he started seeing Luigi and sensing that he's not alone. He believes this all started at a campsite in Arizona in the winter of 1992.

Dan, who partly owned the Toltec Mine at the time, traveled to Quartzsite, AZ, for the annual rock, gem, and mineral trade show to sell his haul of the gem Rhodinite. While staying at a local campground, he was bitten by a poisonous spider and was found unconscious in his tent by a concerned colleague.

Dan woke up two days later in a medical clinic with a stunned doctor by his side. The doctor said, "When you were brought in here, you were basically dead. With the amount of poison that was running through you, I can't believe you're still alive!"

Confused, but happy to be alive, Dan recalled a strange dream.

"I remember a lady dressed in white outside my tent window talking to me," he said.

Grand Imperial Hotel   Silverton

Although he didn't remember exactly what the woman said, she kept talking to him until help arrived. "She kept me going, so I wouldn't die," Dan believed.

He also remembers three dark, shadowy figures standing behind the woman in white. It looked like three men leaning against the fence in black cowboy boots, hats, and glasses. As the four of them left, one of the men tipped his hat and said, "See ya, Dan!"

Thinking it was all just a very strange dream, he kept it to himself. Believing in this sort of thing just wasn't Dan's style. After losing a brother in Vietnam and countless friends to other tragedies, Dan didn't believe in God, and if God did exist, "I hated him," he said.

All that was about to change. Three weeks later Dan was back home in Silverton, CO, when two women stopped by to see him. Although Dan had never met the pair, they said they knew him through a mutual friend. During their conversation one of the women mentioned that she could read palms. Being polite, Dan obliged and offered his hand.

Grand Imperial Hotel   Silverton

The woman pointed to Dan's palm and said, "You died recently and were visited by a woman and three men, right?"

Dan was absolutely shocked. He had told no one of his near-death experience or his dream. His jaw dropped. Then he quietly muttered, "Yeah, how did you know?"

"Actually, I had a dream the other night about your whole ordeal, and I was compelled to come talk to you," she stated. "I just wanted to read your palm so I could get you talking about what happened. Do you know who those three men were?" she asked.

"I think the woman was my guardian angel 'cause she saved my life, and the men behind her had to be . . . angels in training?" Dan surmised.

"Wrong!" she declared. Actually, Dan was half right. "The woman was the one being trained to be an angel by the other three," she said. "And the other three were the Father, Son, and Holy Spirit. It was really important to them that you know who they are; that's why I came."

In Christian circles this trio is known as the Holy Trinity and refers to God, Jesus, and the spirit or wisdom of God. This whole experience changed Dan's outlook, and

## Grand Imperial Hotel	Silverton

he now firmly believes in God and the afterlife. "I know I have spirits looking out for me," he stated. "That's why I see Luigi now, but I couldn't before."

As for his conversations with the lady in white, at the time Dan couldn't remember anything they had talked about. However, as time goes on, things will happen in Dan's life, and suddenly his memory is jogged.

Dan said, "And then I'll say to myself, 'Oh! that's what she meant!'"

Grand Imperial Hotel   **Silverton**

A Titanic Connection

    Before a mined gem or mineral can be sold, it needs to be authenticated for content and purity. When Dan took what he thought was standard Rhodinite to be analyzed, he got a surprising result.

    The pink mineral's unusual content made it unique enough to warrant a new name. Dan, along with the other mine owners, decided to name the beautiful new mineral Astorite after the Toltec mine's former owner, John Astor. Astor was an extremely wealthy and famous businessman who died on the Titanic.

Colorado Map

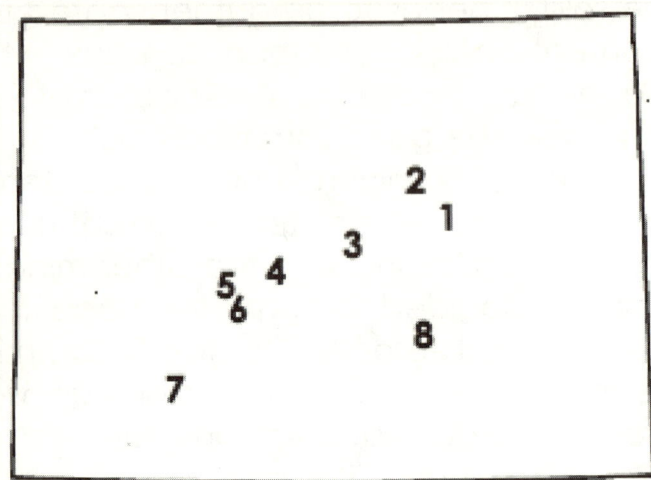

Map Key:

	City	Page #
1	Denver	57
2	Boulder	19
3	Breckenridge	35
4	Aspen	7
5 & 6	Redstone	71
7	Silverton	89
8	Cripple Creek	45

About the Author

This is Sandy Arno Lyons' second book. Her first book, Michigan's Most Haunted: A Ghostly Guide to the Great Lakes State, features ghost stories from around her home state of Michigan.

Although she was born and raised in Michigan, she travels to Colorado frequently to visit family & friends. Currently she lives in Berkley, Michigan, with her family. She is a figure skating coach, author, and mom.

To find out the latest updates on upcoming titles, become a fan on Facebook.